Commander Royal Engineers

The Headquarters of the Royal Engineers at Arnhem

TRAVELOGUE 219

John Sliz

MGES-8 `Commander Royal Engineers, The Headquarters of the Royal Engineers at Arnhem', June 2013
Published by: Travelogue 219
                  Toronto, Canada
ISBN 978-1-927679-04-3

Unless otherwise noted, all charts and drawings by John Sliz

Front cover photo credits: Philip Reinders.

Thank you to Michael Green, Philip Reinders,
and Laura Sliz.

It is my best intention to honour the men of the
Royal Engineers by accurately recording
their accomplishments. If you think that I have misquoted
anyone, gotten anything wrong or have more information
please let me know via my website.

www.stormboatkings.ca

Contents

Glossary

Bde.	Brigade
Capt.	Captain
C.E.	Chief Engineer.
Class 9	A designation for a bridge that can take loads up to and including 9 tons (ie. most medium trucks and cars)
CO	Commanding officer
Col.	Colonel
Coy	Company
CRE	Commander Royal Engineers
Cwt	Hundredweight
Div	Division
DUKW	An amphibious truck
F.B.E.	Folding Boat Equipment mostly used for bridging, but was able to transport infantry
Fd Pk	Field Park
GHQ	General Headquarters
GSO	General Staff Officer
H-hour	Time of attack
Hp	Horse Power
HQ	Headquarters
Hrs	Hours
Lt	Lieutenant
Lt-Col.	Lieutenant Colonel
Maj	Major
M.E.X.E.	Military Engineering Experimental Establishment
m.p.h.	Miles per hour
RAF	Royal Air Force
R.C.E.	Royal Canadian Engineers
Recce	Reconnaissance
RE/R.E.	Royal Engineers
Sapper	The equivalent to a Private in the Engineer Corps
SORE	Staff Officer Royal Engineers

Introduction

At two different times, two men commanded the British 1st Airborne Division's Royal Engineers (R.E.) from their inception to the Battle of Arnhem. It was a coincidence that they both – one, the current Commander, Royal Engineers (CRE) at the time of the Battle of Arnhem and the other a former CRE – not only met during the battle, but worked together to try to relieve the division. Ironically, Lieutenant Colonel Mark Henniker, the CRE who raised and trained the R.E. before he was asked to leave the division, was the man who planned the evacuation. The other, Lieutenant Colonel Eddie Myers, as the senior engineer of the division, was involved with almost all aspects of the division's struggle and because things were going wrong the R.E. had to perform several tasks that weren't in the original plans. One responsibility that dropped onto their shoulders was the job of ferrying the Polish Brigade across the river, you will see, for which he and his men were unequipped. Due to the extraordinary efforts by one of their officers, more men were ferried across than thought possible.

Unlike the other books in this series, this project doesn't focus primarily on one unit during the nine days at Arnhem. Instead, it is from the viewpoint of the senior engineer and of those in his headquarters. It takes into account all of the Royal Engineers under the division as the events unfolded.

Compiled from personal accounts, war diaries, reports and a selected bibliography, this is the story of the chief engineer and his headquarters (HQ) during Operation Market Garden.

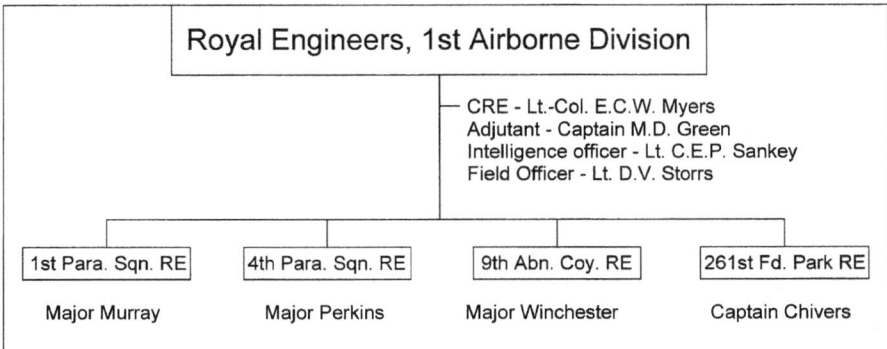

Royal Engineers, 1st Airborne Division

CRE - Lt.-Col. E.C.W. Myers
Adjutant - Captain M.D. Green
Intelligence officer - Lt. C.E.P. Sankey
Field Officer - Lt. D.V. Storrs

1st Para. Sqn. RE	4th Para. Sqn. RE	9th Abn. Coy. RE	261st Fd. Park RE
Major Murray	Major Perkins	Major Winchester	Captain Chivers

The Formation of the Division's Engineers

At the time of the creation of the 1st Airborne Division, the Chief Engineer of HQ Home Forces was Major General B.K. Young and he was responsible for appointing the CRE for this new type of division. He remembered that when he was a Colonel in 1937, he had an adjutant, named Mark Henniker, who he was suitably impressed with. Years later, he thought that he was suitable for the job of CRE of the new airborne division so he recommended to Major General "Boy" Browning, the Officer Commanding (OC) of the 1st Airborne Division at the time, that he was the man for the job. This recommendation came despite Mark Henniker only being an acting Major at the time.[1]

Lieutenant-Colonel Mark Henniker took command in October 1941 and since he occupied only the fourth office to be filled in the new divisional headquarters, his claim that he was in from the start rings true. He was commissioned to build the engineers from the ground up. One of his first tasks was to structure the division's engineers. Because he was given a blank slate, and as there was no precedent, he needed answers to a few questions. One question was what would sappers do in battle and, as the units under his command began to assemble, he asked this question to Stephen Dorman (OC of the 1st Parachute Squadron, R.E. at the time). At first he answered that he didn't know, but then he added, *"Nobody knows, but it will have to be done with very little equipment."* [2]

The new CRE didn't like that answer and when Richard Gale (OC of 1st Parachute Brigade at the time) asked him the same question, Mark Henniker repeated Stephan Dorman's answer and added that he felt it was totally wrong. Gale agreed that the sappers would never have much equipment and that he had plenty to think about. This tied directly in with the first task of the CRE and that was to make recommendations for the establishment and equipment for the engineer component of the division, and then get the War Office to agree to them. After that he had to collect the troops and equipment and following that, training. All of this hinged around the central question, 'what do Airborne Sappers do?'

At the time there were two conflicting views and they both reflected the different roles that people thought the airborne was all about. If the airborne were to be used in small groups then

Right: Lieutenant-Colonel Mark Henniker in 1954.

(Mark Henniker)

Below: King George IV talks with Lt-Colonel Henniker and Major Chivers during an inspectsion of the 261st Field Park Company, R.E.

(Mark Henniker)

Headquarters, Airborne Divisional Engineers War Establishment

(i) Personnel

Commander, R.E. (lieutenant-colonel)	1
Adjutant (captain)	1
Intelligence officer (subaltern)	1
Total officers	3
Tradesman -	
Clerks (includes 1 serjeant)	3
Draughtsman (topographical)	1
Pioneers for duty as -	
Motor-cyclists	2
Total tradesmen (includes 1 lance-corporal)	6
Non-tradesman -	
Drivers, I.C. for duty as -	
Drivers of vehicles	3
Batmen	2
Batman-driver	1
Total, non-tradesmen (includes 1 lance-corporal)	6
Total, other ranks	12
Total, headquarters airborne divisional engineers	15

(ii) Transport

	Airborne	Base
Bicycle	0	1
Bicycle, folding	2	0
Motor-cycles, folding	2	0
Motor-cycles, heavy	0	4
Car, 4-seater, 4x2	0	1
Cars, 5-cwt, 4x4	2	0
Truck, 15-cwt, 4x2, G.S.	0	1
Trailers, 10-cwt	2	0

(iii) Weapons

Pistols, .45-inch, automatic	5
Rifles, .303-inch	10
Anti-tank rifle, .55-inch	1

Above: the war establishment of the Royal Engineers headquarters as of March 1943. The first noticeable difference from the war establishment that went to Arnhem was that a Field Officer hadn't been included yet. Add a Field Engineer and his batman and this is most likely the establishment at Arnhem.

Above: Lt-Col. Henniker is in the middle of the front row with Lt. Sankey (with puppy) to his left and Lt. Storrs to his left. On the CRE's right is Captain Green with Sgt. Cooper to his right. In October 1943, Major Michael D. Green was appointed adjutant to the C.R.E. Sapper Brimble is in the back row on the left. The photo was most likely taken early in 1944 before Henniker was sacked. L/Cpl. Lowe and Sapper Meek are also in the photo, but would leave with the Lt-Col. before Arnhem.
(courtesy of Philip Reinders)

the sapper's role would be almost entirely sabotage, demolition and destruction. Conversely, if the airborne were to land as a division then the sapper's role would be that of a conventional division and would entail building bridges, landing grounds and roads; laying and lifting mines; water supply; and possibly demolition.

Mark Henniker leaned towards the latter and when he spoke with General Browning, he agreed that the engineers must be prepared to operate in the divisional role and then added that the only difference between the airborne sappers and those in a conventional division was how they got to battle. Henniker agreed and then realized that to arrive by parachute and/or in gliders required specially designed and lighter equipment so that was the next task at hand.[3]

Gradually, under Lieutenant-Colonel Henniker, the 1st Parachute Squadron, 4th Parachute Squadron, 9th Field Company and the 261st Field Park Company, R.E. were either formed or joined the division where they were molded and trained to become the division's engineers.[4]

Above both pages: a split photo (with General Urquhart and three others in both sides) of the headquarters of the British 1st Airborne Division taken in July 1944. In the front row fourth from the right with his arms folded is Lt-Col. Henniker. In the back row third from the left is Captain Green. Two over from him is Lt. Storrs. Second from the right in the back row is Lt. Sankey.

Seated between General Urquhart and Lt.-Col. Henniker is Lieutenant-Colonel Robin Goldsmith of the DCLI. He was General Staff Officer 1 of the division when General Urquhart took over. He became the Deputy Chief of Staff HQ 1st Allied Airborne Army and was soon replaced by Charles Mackenzie of the Queen's Own Cameron Highlanders.

Left side: Front row l to r: Lt.-Col. F. Jebens GSO 1 Liaison, Lt-Col. GA Mobbs ADOS, Lt-Col. Kinvig CRÈME, LT-Col. FPHHH Preston AA & QMG, Col. GM Warack ADMS and Maj. General RE Urquhart.

Second row: Maj R Coombe SFGCM, Maj BA Wilson 21 Ind Para Coy, Maj HP Maguire GS02 (Int), Maj JE Miller DADMS, Maj HJA Richards DADH, Maj OP Haig, Maj OF Newton-Dunn. GS02 (Ops).

Third row: Maj JR Halls Transport, Capt RE Bunzley Catering, Capt D Straw SC A, Capt NL Edge Education, Capt M Snowball Camp Commandant, Capt CP Scott-Malden GS03 (Int), Capt JE Killick 89 Fd Sec .

Fourth row: Capt E Arnsby APTC, Lt Morris APO, Capt M Green HQRE, Capt JD Naylor RASC, Lt. DV Storrs HQRE.

Right side: Front row l to r: Maj. General RE Urquhart, Lt-Col. RFK Goldsmith GSO 1 (Ops), Lt-Col MCA Henniker CRE, Lt-Col TGV Stephenson CR Signals, Lt-Col M StJ Packe CRASC, Maj CFH Gough 1 Recce Sqn.

Second row: Maj OF Newton-Dunn GS02 (Ops), Maj PT Tower BRMA, Maj AWH Harlow SCP, Maj LK Hardman DAAG, Sqn Ldr F Whitehouse COC Pilot, Maj ER Hodges DAQMG, Maj DJ Madden GS02 (Air).

Third row: Capt JE Killick 89 Fd Sec, Capt WE Titmuss EME Tels, Capt PVC Sommerville GS03 (Int), Capt Conventry SC Q, Cpat GC Grieve GS03 (Ops), Capt AE Ewens EME, Capt OC Roberts ADC to GOC.

Fourth row: Lt DV Storrs, Lt CH Barber, Lt Drake, Lt PRR de Burgh HQRA, Lt CEP Sankey HQRE, Lt AD Butterworth HQ Def.

Change of Command

Whether there were complaints about Lieutenant-Colonel Henniker or not, or if General Urquhart wanted to exercise his authority over the old guard in the division, he decided that the CRE had to go. It is interesting that the General fails to mention this event in his autobiography, suggesting that he considered it to be a very minor hiccup in the history of the division.

During the last few months before his termination, Mark Henniker did not possess the same optimistic spirit that had infected the division where nobody wanted to rock the boat by saying why a plan wouldn't work. He mentions the following in his memoirs, *"We studied a great many possible and impossible operations, and I found myself gradually getting more and more out of step with those I was working with. Never in my career had I been a "Yes-man". If anyone had asked my opinion on any of our plans my "gut reaction" would have been to reply: "Have nothing to do with it". Luckily no one did ask me my opinion, but I'm sure most of them felt that they would do better with another man in my place. I felt in my own heart that I was becoming a "bolshie officer". General Urquhart must have been aware of this too, though we never had a cross word. Exactly how it came about I do not know, but on 10 August he said to me, "I think that you've been too long in this Airborne business. You've been Airborne for nearly three years and it's time you had an innings with an Infantry Division in Normandy. I'll help you to get a decent appointment in 21 Army Group, but will you tell me which of these Sappers I've been offered in your place is the best one?"* [5]

On the list that Mark Henniker was shown, he thought that Lieutenant-Colonel Eddie Myers was the best choice as he had known him for years and thought of him as, *"a most accomplished man. Before the War he had, among other things, been a most successful Point-to-Point rider; he was also a well-qualified engineer, very shrewd in outlook, and had recently been in Greece, having been dropped there by parachute to assist the Partisans. He was an obvious choice for CRE 1 Airborne Division."* [6]

Myers had been so highly regarded that he had been interviewed by Churchill and Eden, the Foreign Secretary, when he got back to England.

Fortunately when Lieutenant-Colonel Edmund Myers took command of the British 1st Airborne Division's engineers in August 1944, the ground work had already been done by his predecessor, Colonel Mark Henniker. Unfortunately, for Myers, he had very little time to get himself acquainted with his new command before they flew to Arnhem to face their toughest challenge. He had two nicknames. The first one was 'Eddie' after the famous footballer Eddie Myers, and the second was 'Tito' because he had served with the partisans. The fact that he had served with the partisans in Greece and not Yugoslavia did not matter to whoever gave him this nickname.[7]

Lieutenant-Colonel Myers: *"The first seven days I was fully occupied, staying in turn with my units which were scattered widely throughout LINCOLNSHIRE and adjoin counties. (I had to cover 150 miles to visit the four of them.) The remainder of the time was spent in planning three abortive operations at Airborne Corps Headquarters near RICHMANSWORTH. I knew only a few of my officers; I knew practically none of my men. But, fortunately for the Division, Lieutenant Colonel M.C.A. Henniker, DSO OBE MC RE, my predecessor, had brought into existence and trained four RE units which were an immediate pride to command."* [8]

Left: Lieutenant-Colonel Edmund Myers.

Middle: Lieutenant Sankey.
(Philip Reinders)

Right: Lieutenant Storrs
(Philip Reinders)

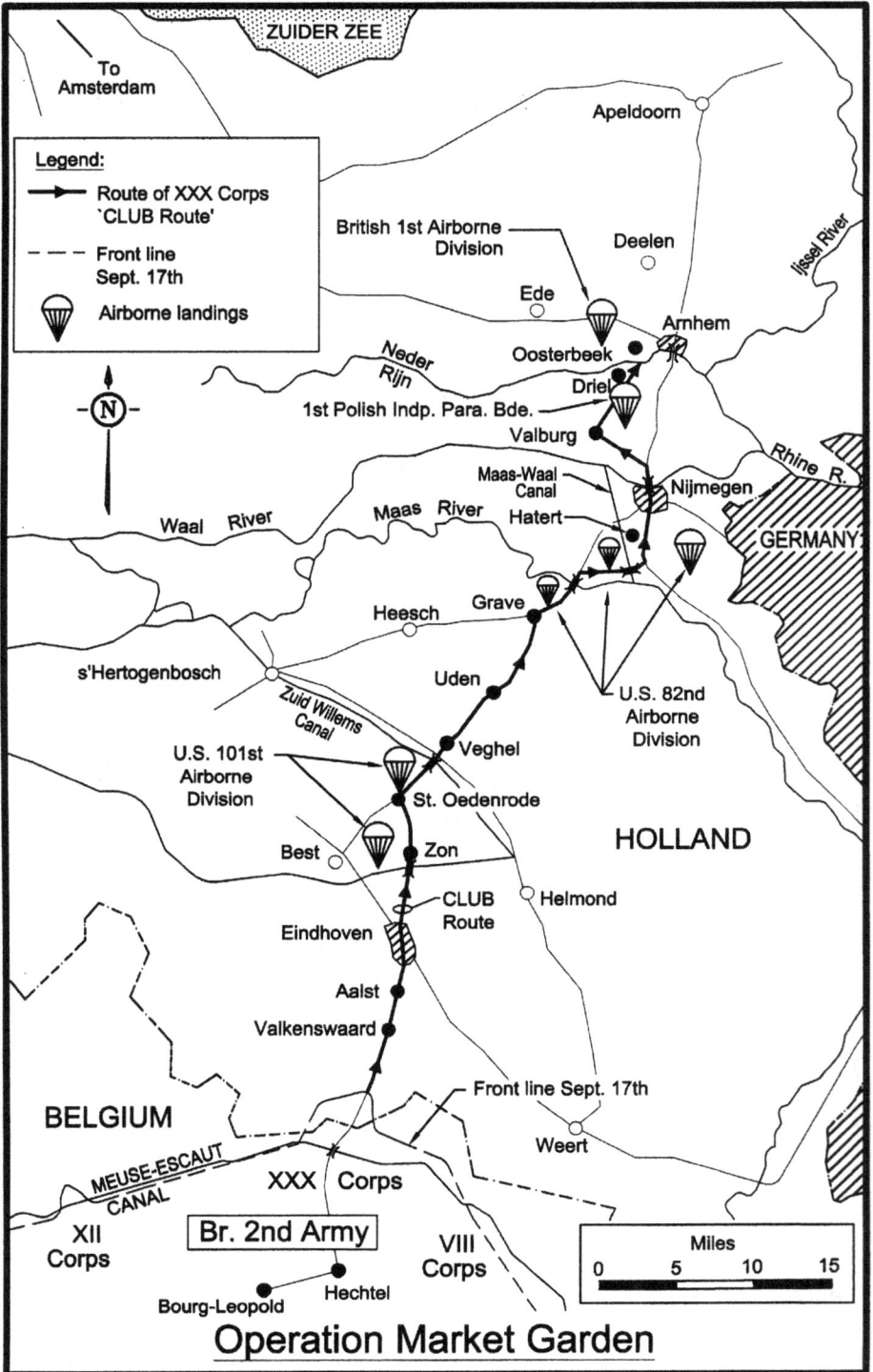

Operation Market Garden

Operation Market Garden

When the Allies broke out of Normandy at the end of the summer in 1944 they were chasing the enemy back to Germany and as a result of this pursuit, numerous airborne operations were planned to exploit this advantage to try to bring a swift end to the war. As the Allied armies made their way through France and into Belgium, the newly created 1st Allied Airborne Army was sitting in the UK waiting to be used. Field Marshal Montgomery came up with a plan that would use this resource by dropping three of its divisions behind the German lines. They were to capture all of the bridges over the river and canals of The Netherlands and to clear a path for the British 2nd Army to outflank the West Wall and into Germany.

This plan, known as Operation Market Garden, was for the US 101st Airborne Division, the US 82nd Airborne Division and the British 1st Airborne Division with the 1st Independent Polish Parachute Brigade to land by parachute and glider behind the front line and for XXX Corps to break through the front line and drive up the road, relieving each division in turn. It was hoped that they would reach the furthest division, the British 1st Airborne Division, within two to three days and that they would have captured at least one of the three bridges across the Neder Rijn or Rhine River.

Unfortunately, because of a shortage of transport aircraft it would take three lifts to bring the entire division and the Polish brigade into Arnhem. Also, the area where the division was to land was far from the bridges and because of this, a *coup de main* assault by the Recce Squadron, supported by a small group of engineers, were to capture the main bridge in Arnhem.

The division's defense of Arnhem was for the 1st Parachute Brigade to hold the area north and south of the main road and pontoon bridges and for the other three brigades to hold the north side of the river, including Arnhem and the railway bridge. They would be from west to east: the 1st Air Landing Brigade, the 4th Parachute Brigade and the 1st Polish Independent Brigade. In this configuration, the division would be in a strong defensive position to hold out until the arrival of XXX Corps.

The Engineer's Plan

Operational instructions were issued on September 12th based on Lieutenant-Colonel Myers' verbal orders (which became `CRE 1 Airborne Div Op. Instruction No. 1') and the report went into detail of what was required from the Royal Engineers at Arnhem. The overall primary tasks were to seize intact and hold in order of importance: the main road bridge in Arnhem, the pontoon bridge and the railway bridge. The engineers were to assist in the capture of these bridges by means of flame-throwers, Bangalore torpedoes, pole charges and by neutralizing and removing any demolition charges.

The secondary tasks were to assist in the subsequent defense of the bridges, block all road and railway approaches to Arnhem from all directions, to relocate all ferries, barges, boats and tugs to the north bank of the River Rijn and the west bank of Ijssel. Also, they were to guard and supervise the power station, the waterworks and gas works and if necessary to operate a ferry. An RE Stores Dump for resupply and captured equipment was to be operated, the operation of the railway, if necessary, and general brigade defensive tasks, such as loop holing and other building preparations.

In support of the 1st Parachute Brigade, upon landing the 1st Parachute Squadron, R.E. and two detachments of the 9th Field Company, R.E. were placed under the brigade's command and were to remain there until the arrival of the second lift. The two detachments of the 9th Field Company, R.E. were attached to the Recce Squadron and were to assist in the capture of the road and pontoon bridge by neutralizing and removing all enemy demolition charges. Then they were to help hold the bridge until the arrival of the 1st Parachute Brigade.

Upon arrival of the second lift, the 1st Parachute Squadron, R.E., less one troop remaining under command of the 1st Parachute Brigade for defense and other local tasks, reverted to be under the command of the CRE and was to rendezvous at the Power Station, and the two detachments of 9th Field Company, R.E. reverted to under command OC of 9th Field Company, R.E. and were to rendezvous at Tafellaan.

One platoon of 9th Field Company and the detachment of 261 Field Park Company, R.E. with the Clarke Crawler was to be placed under the command of the 1st Airlanding Brigade and were to clear all vehicles from the landing zones and help with the brigade defensive tasks. Upon arrival of 4th Parachute Brigade and occupation by 1st Airlanding Brigade's new position, they were to place road and railway blocks from the north, north-west and west.

When the second lift arrived with the 4th Parachute Brigade, the 4th Parachute Squadron, R.E. were to remain under their control until the arrival of the Polish Parachute Brigade on the third lift. During this time they were to assist the 4th onto its objectives and then to take over from the 1st Parachute Squadron, R.E. the road blocks to Arnhem from the north and northeast. On arrival of the Polish Parachute Brigade, the 4th Parachute Squadron, R.E., less one troop remained under command of 4th Parachute Brigade for local tasks, was to come under the control of the CRE and concentrate at the railway station.

On arrival on the first day, the CRE would have under command the 9th Field Company, R.E. (less one troop permanently under command of the 1st Airlanding Brigade and the two detachments under the command of the 1st Parachute Brigade). One detachment was to seize and hold the railway bridge and remove demolition charges and to make a temporary cut of the railway line from the south. Interesting that no orders were made for this detachment if the railway bridge had been blown. The HQRE and the remainder of the field company were to rendezvous at Tafallaan and be prepared to operate ferries between the railway bridge and pontoon bridge.

The detachment of the 261st Field Park Company, R.E. (less the Clarke Crawler detachment) was to operate RE stores (resupply and captured stores) and concentrate at RE Stores Dump.

If the bridges had all been blown then the squadron's tasks would be the following: they were to seize all ferries, barges, boats and tugs so they could be used by XXX Corps. They were to recce for six Class 40 raft sites, one standard floating Bailey bridge Class 40 and one floating Bailey Barge Bridge Class 40. All of the equipment and manpower for these bridges was with 2nd Army's engineers and would arrive on a predetermined schedule.* The 1st Parachute Squadron, R.E. was also to prepare for the conversion of the railway bridge to maximum class road vehicles and were to give special attention to approaches for bridges, carrying out preliminary work in this respect if time and engineer resources permitted. It is considered that three approaches off the main axis would be sufficient, i.e. one for the six rafting site, one for Bailey pontoon site, and one for Bailey barge site. The approach roads should diverge at a sufficient distance from the main site to prevent traffic congestion and delay near the crossings.

A future task was to recce the Waal River at Nijmegen for Bailey bridges for XXX Corps and subsequent maintenance of all Bailey bridges in the Arnhem and Nijmegen area.

The minimal equipment to be taken by all the engineering units of the division was by unit:

> 1500 lbs of explosives
> 12 Beehives
> 2 rope ladders per troop
> 2 pairs of gym shoes per troop
> 50 mines, Anti-tank, Mark V
> 2 Hawkins Grenades per man
> 6 Flame Throwers

In addition, the 261st Field Park, RE took a Clarke Crawler and three jeeps with trailers containing each: 25 anti-tank mines or 100 Hawkins Grenades, 300 pounds of explosives and fifteen personnel mines. The 9th Field Company, R.E. also brought three compressor trailers with them.

All units were to issue daily situation reports as of 1700 hours and they were due to reach the CRE by any means by 1900 hours, and a brief overnight situation report as of 0730 hours by wireless was due to reach the CRE by 0800 hours. Also, upon arrival on the landing or drop zone, the attached liaison officer or NCO was to report to HQRE as soon as possible.

HQRE was to be located in area of TAC 1st Airborne Division Artillery Park and arrange the resupply with 261st Field Park Company, R.E. with jeeps and trailers.[9]

Three days later, on behalf of Lt-Col. Myers, Lieutenant C.E.P.

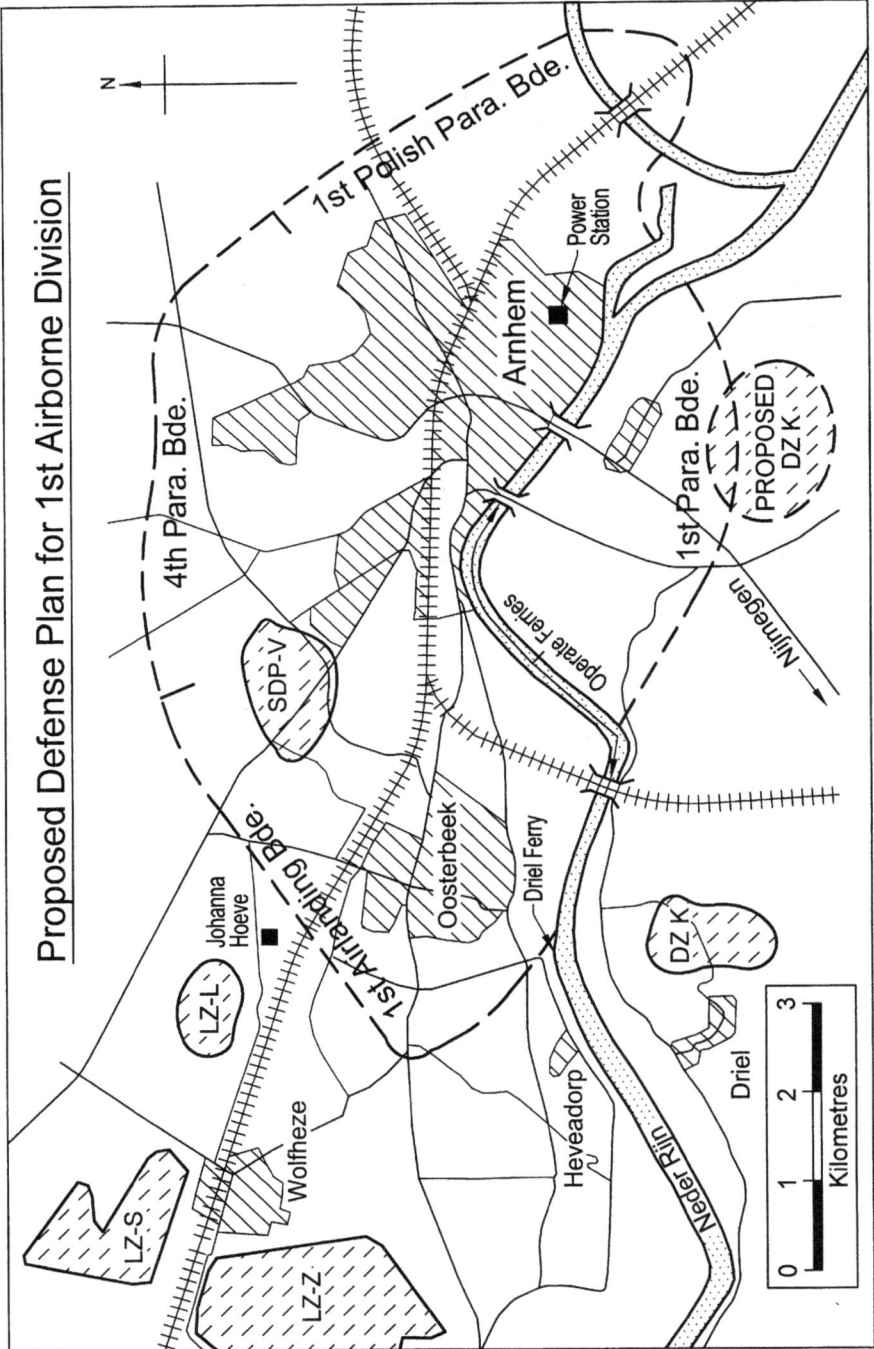

Proposed Defense Plan for 1st Airborne Division

Sankey made a few changes (which have already been changed above) and added a few more items to the original report. The first item that was added was that no bridges were to be destroyed or prepared for destruction and that temporary minor rail cuts may be made for the purpose of local defense. No demolitions of any kind, and no destruction of signal communications (except German Field Cable) were to be allowed. 1st Parachute Brigade, would, however, ensure that the Arnhem signal exchange was disconnected.

The only mines to be laid were to be under RE supervision to ensure accurate recording. Own and enemy minefields were to be reported through normal channels by the quickest possible means, and in the case of enemy minefields also to the nearest RE unit.

The friendly Dutch civilians properly enrolled for labour through the Civil Affairs mission were issued with blue and white armbands as worn by the Dutch Resistance.[10]

1st Lift September 17th

At 1038 hours, 190 Squadron RAF took off from Fairford airfield and ten Stirling bombers towing ten gliders (chalk numbers 431 to 440) carried the Divisional headquarters that included the CRE. Simultaneously, 299 Squadron RAF took off from Keevil Airfield and its sixteen Striling bombers towing sixteen gliders (chalk numbers 381 to 396), carried part of the headquarters of the Royal Engineers. This glider carried a jeep, a trailer, and a motorcycle along with the Field Engineer, D.V. Storrs and a few men from HQRE. The total number of men and officers for HQRE on the first lift was three officers and eight men. Officially there wasn't a Field Engineer on the establishment of the HQRE of the British 1st Airborne Division and it was added ad hoc. Before being attached to the CRE Lieutenant David Storrs was part of the 9th Field Company.[14]

Despite doing a large number of parachute jumps, one of them in connection with an operation behind enemy lines in the Balkans, Lieutenant-Colonel Myers had never been in a glider before. With him in his glider, that contained a jeep and trailer, were the following personnel: his Intelligence Officer, Lieutenant Crofton E. Peter Sankey, Chief Clerk Sergeant Cooper, Driver Hill, Sapper Vincent Hagan Brimble (Clerk/Radio Operator), a Dutch interpreter from No. 10 Commando, and a medical orderly. Lieutenant-Colonel Myers: *"For the best part of an hour we circled over the West of England behind the Halifax which was our tug, gradually gaining height and waiting until it was time to rendezvous in the air over the Midlands. It was a clear bright morning and in the distance I could see the hills of Exmoor, and my home, as we once circled over the Bristol Channel. Eventually, after what seemed an interminable time, we set our course Eastwards for the coast of Essex. As we left what appeared below us as a peaceful sunlit England, the spectacle in the air all around us was enthralling. Ahead of us, around us and behind us, as far as the eye could see, the air was full of aircraft tugging gliders, and to one flank a stream of faster aircraft, Dakotas, carrying parachutists, was already beginning to overtake us."*[15]

Over the channel, one of the pilots beckoned Lt-Colonel Myers forward into the cockpit and pointed out in the sea below them was a Halifax and its glider. They could see in the distance an

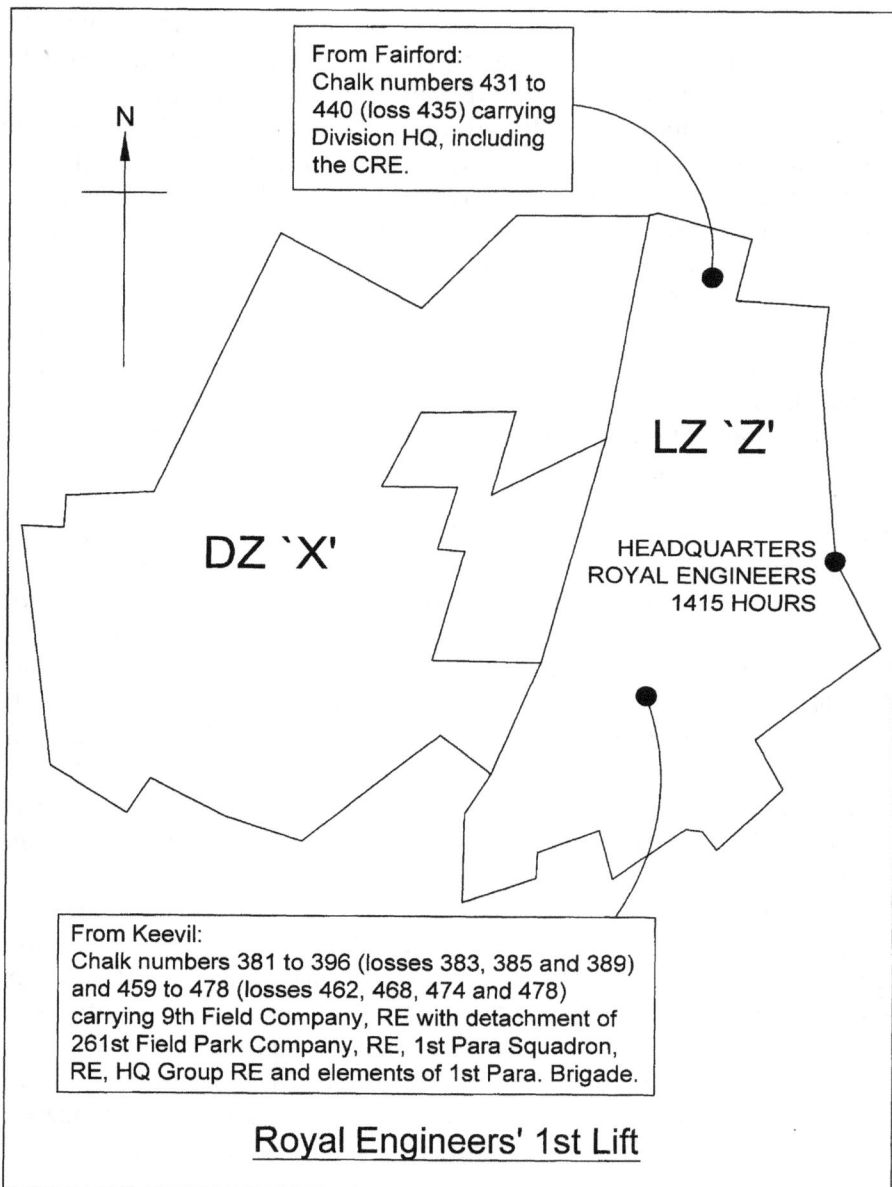

N

From Fairford:
Chalk numbers 431 to
440 (loss 435) carrying
Division HQ, including
the CRE.

LZ `Z'

DZ `X'

HEADQUARTERS
ROYAL ENGINEERS
1415 HOURS

From Keevil:
Chalk numbers 381 to 396 (losses 383, 385 and 389)
and 459 to 478 (losses 462, 468, 474 and 478)
carrying 9th Field Company, RE with detachment of
261st Field Park Company, RE, 1st Para Squadron,
RE, HQ Group RE and elements of 1st Para. Brigade.

Royal Engineers' 1st Lift

air-sea rescue launch already making its way, at top speed, towards the downed plane and glider and their unfortunate occupants. These weren't the only 'ditched' aircraft and gliders. Once they reached Holland they saw the devastation the Germans had created. Here and there a small village, a road or a railway on an embankment, stood up above the flooded land. Scattered amongst the flooded land were enemy anti-aircraft batteries and as their flak came close, RAF fighter bombers finished them off. Only one glider from either group, chalk number 435, was lost on the way, but it didn't carry anyone from the HQRE.[16]

Near the landing zone, Lieutenant-Colonel Myers felt a heavy jerk. *"We slowed down; the noise of the air rushing past the glider ceased, and we silently started to float down to earth. We were all strapped in. The pilot put the nose of the glider down and we dived towards the ground at a great speed. When within a hundred feet of it, he flattened out the machine, to make a perfect landing in a huge field of potatoes."* [17]

Sapper Brimble described the journey to the Netherlands as uneventful and their landing in a cabbage field near Wolfheze like landing on Southhampton Common. In other words, good. The first task upon landing was to release the bolts on the tail of the glider to unload the motorcycle and jeep. This Sergeant Cooper and Sapper Brimble found difficult as the control lines were obstructing the process. An axe was used to cut these, giving access to the bolts.[18]

At 1335 hours, both gliders landed on Landing Zone 'Z'. The CRE, IORE, Field Engineer and eight other ranks from HQRE all arrived safely. Nearby on the trapezoid-shaped field directly alongside the Wolfheze woods, a Hamilcar overturned and killed one pilot and trapped the other. Digging the earth beneath him only caused the glider to shift. Lieutenant-Colonel Myers was frustrated because he didn't have a block and tackle to release the trapped pilot. Eventually a carrier was used to lift the glider off him.[19]

Lieutenant-Colonel Myers: *"Apart from a few rifle shots and crackling of burning woodwork of houses in the trees towards Wolfhezen – the result of preliminary air bombing – all was silent. It was difficult to realize that we were fifty miles in advance of our own troops, in enemy occupied Holland. I had only my Intelligence Officer, Lieutenant Peter Sankey, my Chief Clerk and one*

DR, together with my driver and our Headquarters jeep and trailer, in my glider. But my Field Engineer, Lieutenant David Storrs, soon joined me from another one. The rest of the Airborne element of HQRE was due to arrive the following day." [20]

The HQRE was set up in the nearby woods and was up and running by 1415 hours at 658797. Here they endured a mortar attack, dug in and spent the night. Sapper Brimble claimed that *"fortunately the soil was sandy and not too difficult to dig in".*[21]

At 1930 hours the HQRE moved to operate from gliders. They spent the first night in or around the gliders on the dropping zone. As tempting as it might have been to check on his units, the CRE remained at headquarters. Myers: *"The situation was too obscure, I thought, to warrant my going off with, at that time, the only jeep of HQRE, to discover the progress of either the sappers of 9 Field Company with the Recce Squadron, 1 Parachute Squadron with 1 Parachute Brigade, or the detachment of 9 Field Company whose task it was to try and seize intact the railway bridge over the Neder Rijn just East of Oosterbeek."* [22]

The 18th and the Second Lift

At 0600 hours the HQRE moved to the edge of the landing zone and then an hour later - as Divisional Headquarters moved into the woods — HQRE moved again to be with them. German fighters appeared at 1115 hours over the landing zone, but the HQRE wasn't hit.[23]

The second lift was scheduled to take off at dawn but due to low cloud and adverse weather conditions did not take off until after mid-day. From Keevil 299 Squadron RAF took off towing gliders (chalk numbers 950-969), circled over the airfield area for about an hour and then made for Aldeburgh where they assembled with the parachute aircraft to cross the Channel.[24]

Captain Green: *"Looking out of the glider I could see aircraft for miles. The three hour flight was reasonably uneventful, except that we all felt very air sick with the bumping of the glider on the airstream of the towing aircraft. Everyone was very relieved when we were informed that the LZ was in sight. We cast off from the towing aircraft about 5 miles from the LZ. There was a eerie silence as the glider dived sharply towards the LZ. I was in the cockpit when we cast off, as we descended all I could see was a large field littered with broken gliders and abandoned parachutes, I could not see how the pilots could possibly find a space to land, I told the men to brace themselves as it could clearly be a bumpy landing. The pilot with great skill touched down rose again over a crashed glider and landed safely on the other side."*
[25]

Once the glider came to a halt the unloading procedure started. The elevator wires were cut to release the four tail bolts so the tail dropped away. Captain Green and the two pilots jumped out of the door and pulled the tail away while the men in the glider un-coupled the jeep and trailer, pushed out the ramp and man-handled the jeep and trailer to the ground. All of this took about seven minutes and there was a considerable amount of gunfire all around them but none seemed to be directed at Captain Green and the other occupants of his glider. They moved quickly to the rendezvous point. When under cover of the woods Captain Green set off a blue flair and the rest of his party soon joined them.

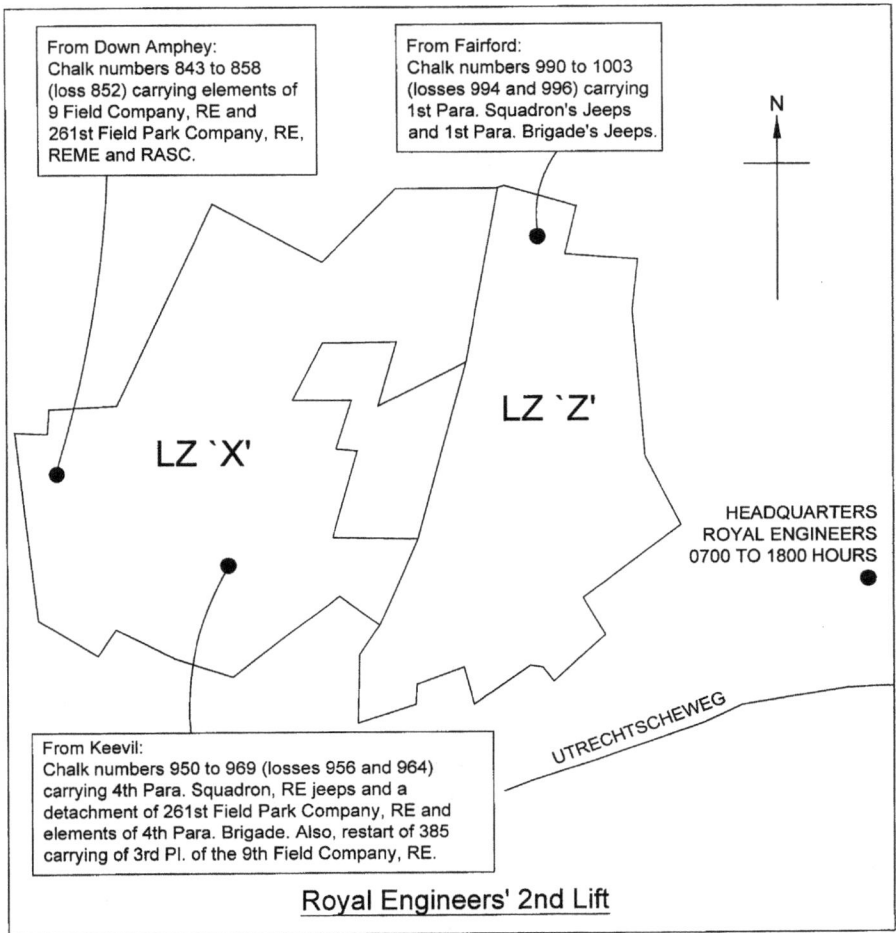

From Down Amphey:
Chalk numbers 843 to 858
(loss 852) carrying elements of
9 Field Company, RE and
261st Field Park Company, RE,
REME and RASC.

From Fairford:
Chalk numbers 990 to 1003
(losses 994 and 996) carrying
1st Para. Squadron's Jeeps
and 1st Para. Brigade's Jeeps.

N

LZ `Z'

LZ `X'

HEADQUARTERS
ROYAL ENGINEERS
0700 TO 1800 HOURS

UTRECHTSCHEWEG

From Keevil:
Chalk numbers 950 to 969 (losses 956 and 964)
carrying 4th Para. Squadron, RE jeeps and a
detachment of 261st Field Park Company, RE and
elements of 4th Para. Brigade. Also, restart of 385
carrying of 3rd Pl. of the 9th Field Company, RE.

Royal Engineers' 2nd Lift

The time was 15:00 hours, five hours later than scheduled.

Captain Green, *"Our small party had arrived intact. We re-organized the loading of our 3 jeeps and trailers, so that we had easy access to our radios and could maintain reasonable fire positions while we moved forward towards Arnhem. Our aim was to avoid contact with the enemy if possible and proceed quickly to Div HQ at Oosterbeek about 5 miles away. It took us 5 hours to do the 5 miles to Oosterbeek arriving just before dark, we quickly made contact with Lt.-Col. Myers who had arrived at the Hartenstein Hotel a few hours before us, which was now established as Div. HQ."* [26]

They arrived at HQRE at 1605. At 18:00 the HQRE moved to

Oosterbeek to set up with the rest of the Divisional HQ in the Hartenstein Hotel. The HQRE was given an area in the grounds about 130 metres from the hotel. There they dug in and found a number of four-inch logs that they used as cover. The HQRE remained there throughout the operation until they were evacuated.[27]

Lieutenant-Colonel Myers got on the radio to Major Murray who was then with the elements of 1st Parachute Brigade on the North end of the bridge. Things weren't going well and with the growing German pressure, plans where changing. There were several attempts to get supplies to the bridge, but all of these were unsuccessful by the German blocking line near the museum. The force at the bridge was holding out well, but was now cut off from the rest of the division.

Unexpected Journeys

At 0930 on the 19th, division headquarters experienced its first mortaring by the enemy. According to Lieutenant-Colonel Myers, *"It was pretty heavy."*[28]

With his sappers spread out from being trapped at the bridge to being pushed off the landing zones, the CRE needed to find out who was where. He already knew that all of his sappers were now fighting as infantry and that things weren't going well. Lieutenant-Colonel Myers: *"Before nightfall, 9 Field Company, already with two officers killed and one missing, and 4 Parachute Squadron, its ranks also considerably depleted as a result of its fight in from the area of the DZs, were both in infantry defensive positions within 200 yards of Divisional Headquarters, to the West and North respectively of the Hartenstein Hotel. The detachment of 261st Field Park Company, its officer, Lieutenant Skinner, killed* (Although he didn't know it at the time, officially the Lieutenant was missing in action)".[29]

To try to establish the position and situation of their troops Captain Green, Peter Sankey and David Storrs were sent out to report on their positions and situations, but unlike Lieutenant Storrs they didn't make contact with the enemy. Lieutenant Storrs, with two other ranks (one sapper and one Dutch guide), went on an offensive patrol to reconnoiter the railway bridge which by then HQRE had heard the party of 9 Field Company, under Captain O'Callaghan's command, had failed to capture intact. The enemy had blown it up in front of their noses just as they were approaching, and O'Callaghan had taken his sappers on with the elements of 1 Parachute Brigade to the main road bridge at Arnhem.[30]

Of those not at the bridge, most of Myers' sappers were gathered around the Sonnenberg, a large house northwest of the Hartenstien. Here half of the 4th Parachute Squadron, RE, most of the 9th Field Company, RE, what was left of the 261st Field Park Company, RE and part of the 1st Parachute Squardon, RE were gathered under the command of Major Winchester. The engineers at the bridge were fighting along with 2nd Battalion, The Parachute Regiment and other elements of 1st Parachute Brigade. They were still holding the bridge but were under consider-

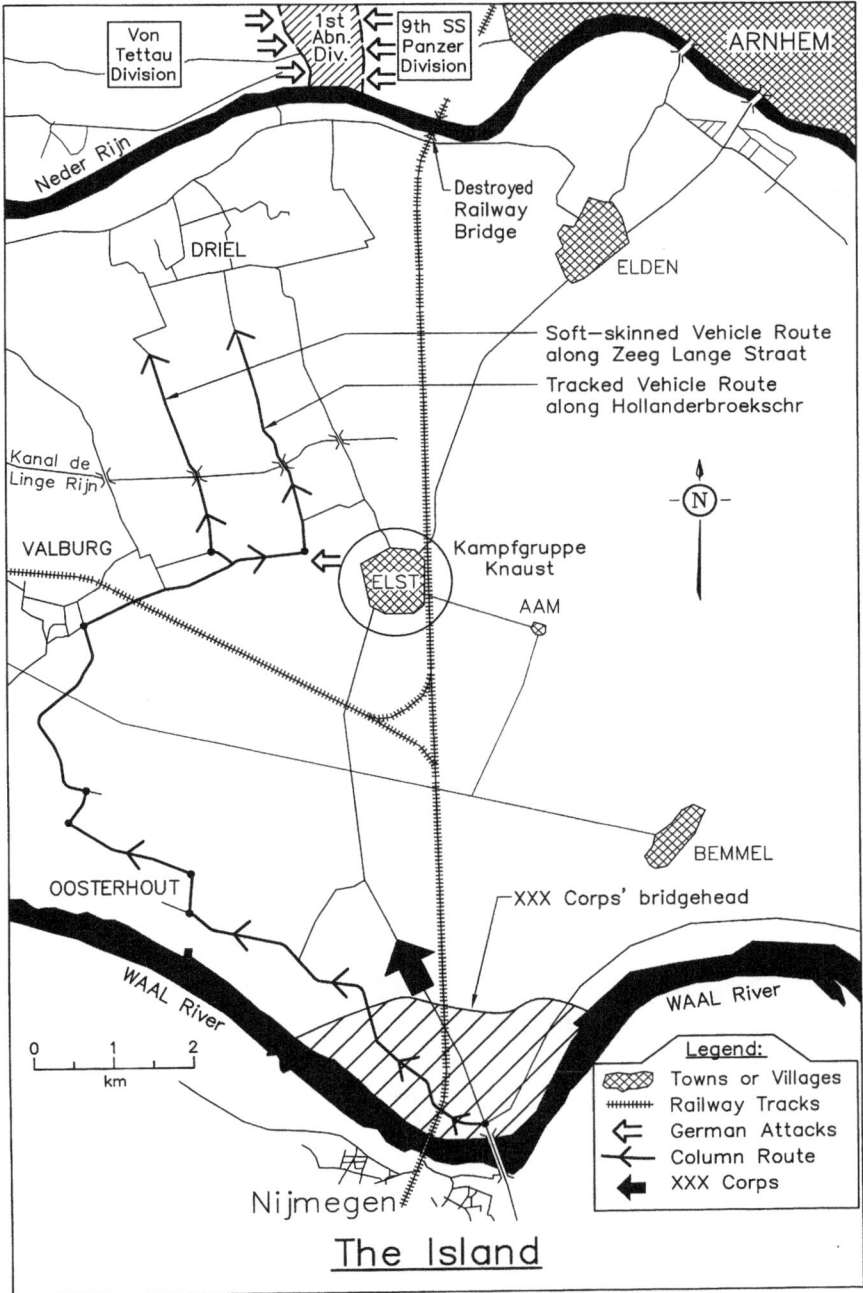

Von Tettau Division

1st Abn. Div.

9th SS Panzer Division

ARNHEM

Neder Rijn

Destroyed Railway Bridge

DRIEL

ELDEN

Soft-skinned Vehicle Route along Zeeg Lange Straat

Tracked Vehicle Route along Hollanderbroekschr

Kanal de Linge Rijn

-N-

VALBURG

ELST

Kampfgruppe Knaust

AAM

BEMMEL

OOSTERHOUT

XXX Corps' bridgehead

WAAL River

WAAL River

Legend:
Towns or Villages
Railway Tracks
German Attacks
Column Route
XXX Corps

0 1 2
km

Nijmegen

The Island

able pressure from the Germans from the South and didn't think they could hold out much longer.

Sapper Brimble was tasked with accompanying Driver Hill, who was to take a message to the forces regrouping at Oosterbeek Church. The journey was hairy, going through the woods where trees were covered with phosperous, which glowed eerily in the dark. At the church Sapper Brimble saw many dead airborne troops outside. He recalls the church being packed with able and wounded airborne troops. The return journey was equally hairy but they arrived safely back at the Hartenstein.[31]

Lieutenant-Colonel Myers instructed 9 Company to send a party down to the ferry at Heaveadorp with instructions to gather up all the river craft they could find to the West and to bring them within the perimeter. Due to the lack of equipment to start the three barges that were found, they couldn't be brought into the perimeter. In Myers' opinion, the presence of steam and diesel engine drivers would have been very useful. The absence of the entire 261st Field Park Company, RE was surely felt.[32]

The morning of the 20th brought pretty intensive shelling and small arms fire around the Divisional Headquarter's area. By now all attempts to get to the bridge had ceased and the formation of the Oosterbeek Perimeter had started the previous afternoon.

Much has been written about the resupply drops by the RAF so I will only add Lieutenant-Colonel Myers' reaction to watching the event: *"The only peace one got from incessant enemy mortaring was when the RAF bravely flew in their "resupply" aircraft. The enemy used to turn everything on to them. But our pilots flew straight on, into and through it all even though the enemy took heavy toll. It made us writhe as we saw them being shot down, and most of our valuable stores floating into the enemy's lines – their sacrifice to no avail."* [33]

Via the Phantom wireless link news was received that XXX Corps had reached Nijmegen so the CRE decided to send off Captain Michael Green to make contact with the Chief Engineer and to give him all the information possible about the river. At 1740 hours Green left with another officer of Divisional Headquarters, GSO I.O. Captain C.P. Scott Malden, G3 Intelligence." [34]

The members of the 9th Field Company, R.E. under the command of Captain Higgins reported that Captain Green arrived safely at 1955 Hours.[35]

Captain Green: *"The ferry was operated by a chain which went over a large pulley on the deck, by winding this pulley the ferry would slowly be pulled across the river. After saying good bye to our escort, we started pulling the ferry across the river, progress was very slow, when we were about two thirds across, the movement of the ferry must have alerted the Germans because they started to fire mortars at us, one shell hit the cable, we lost control and the ferry started drifting downstream, so we had no alternative but to swim for the bank, the current was very fast, my companion drifted downstream and I never saw him again, but I managed to reach the bank. There was one of 4th Para Bde serjeants on the bank who had been on a recce and was trying to get back to his unit. I told him that I had to make my way to Nijmegen, could he give me any information about the enemy positions, he said that he had been in contact with a Dutch family who would help, we looked around for my companion but he was nowhere to be seen, so I asked the Serjeant to come with me as two of us would be more likely to succeed in reaching Nijmegen. The Serjeant took me to the Dutch family he had met in Driel. The two young sons of the Dutch family seemed to know everything about the German positions, which was a great help as Driel was full of German soldiers, by this time it was clear that we would not be able to reach Nijmegen before it got light, so we decided to stay the night with the Dutch family hiding in the basement and would leave early next morning. They fed us and dried my clothes and I was able to get a few hours sleep."* [36]

Just after midnight Captain Green briefed the Sergeant as to the exact position at Oosteerbeek, so that if anything happened to him he could pass on the message to CRE XXX Corps. They were guided by two Dutch boys through the town avoiding any German positions and sent them off over the fields and dikes. Captain Green: *"We could see Nijmegen about 7 miles distance by the fires. We kept well away from any roads scrambling over dikes some of which were quite wide and after about 3 hours we reached the main road through ELST, this was clearly a German defence line as they were dug in all along the road between the houses, we crawled inch by inch through the gardens until we could see the edge of the road, the German positions were all*

Above: the view from the Westerbouwing showing the terrain south of the river. It was over these grounds that Lt-Col Myers and Captain Green had to trasverse. The old ferry site would have been at the bottom of the photograph just on the other side of the trees. (taken by author)

Below: a pre-war photograph of the ferry. Captain Green was to take the last ride. (Geert Maasen)

around us we could hear them talking. It was very dark so we decided bluff was the only answer, we would get up, the Sergeant who spoke German would speak to me and we would walk straight across the road to a gap in the houses opposite. It worked, nobody noticed us, as soon as we were hidden between the houses we waited to see if anyone moved, clearly we had not been seen, so we made our way through the gardens over a field to the woods beyond. We knew that we couldn't be very far from Nijmegen and it was possible that our troops would not be far away, this was very much "no man's land". It was beginning to get light so we had to make for the woods. Just before we reached the woods there was a shout 'Halt' we hopefully replied friend, we were told to advance with our hands up, fortunately they were US troops. They escorted us to their officer in charge, we told our story and they agreed to drive us to Nijmegen." [37]

The time was 0330 hours.

Captain Green and the sergeant were driven to Nijmegen in a jeep and arrived at dawn. To his surprise the first person he met was Lt-Col. Henniker. Captain Green: *"He was very surprised but delighted to see me and immediately took me to his tent and offered me a large whisky, never has a whiskey tasted so good nor ever will. After I explained the situation to him he agreed to set up a meeting with General Horrocks and his staff as soon as possible. In the meanwhile he got his batman to dry and clean my uniform while I got some sleep."* [38]

When Lieutenant-Colonel Henniker left the division, his driver, Lance-Corporal Lowe and his batman, Sapper Meck, both volunteered to come with him and General Urquhart told him to take the jeep. Sadly they sent their prized Red Berets home and headed to Deal, UK. There they crossed in a landing craft to Arromanches on their way the Reinforcement Depot Camp near Bayeux.

Mark Henniker: *"The Base Reinforcement Depot near Bayeux was the nearest approach to Hell on Earth that I had ever seen. There was absolutely nothing to do. Bored officers sat aimlessly in the sunshine, discussing the prospects of languishing there for ever, and because casualties had been mercifully light in comparison with 1914-18, the prospect of a life sentence seemed quite possible."* [39]

In order not to crumble away at the depot, and since he knew both the Chief Engineer of the 21st Army Group and his Deputy, he set out to their headquarters. He had luck and soon he found himself in front of the deputy, General Tickell, who in 1924 was an instructor of his at the Royal Military Academy. Lieutenant-Colonel Henniker was given the task of overseeing the dismantling of all the Bailey bridges that weren't needed and stock piling them at a central location in anticipation of the Germans retreating and blowing all of the bridges all the way to Germany.

Soon after, he found a Posting Order awaiting him. He was instructed to take over as CRE of the 43rd Wessex Infantry Division. The former CRE, Lieutenant-Colonel Pike had been recently wounded in the interim. Major Tom Evill acted as CRE and it was him that represented the division's engineers at General Horrock's famous address on the 16th. Mark Henniker didn't take command until the next day, which was the day that the operation started. It was a lot to take in. He had to learn all of the units and CO under his command, the overall plan for Market / Garden, the engineer plan and more importantly, he had to learn how to deal with the division's commander, Major General G.I. Thomas who was famous for mercilessly ripping a man apart if he thought that his argument was unsound. This set a tone throughout the entire division.[40]

Trapped

Meanwhile, north of the river, the headquarters was down to quarter rations and the enemy mortaring was incessant and heavy. It started about 06:50 on the 21st and around 10:00 the ammunition and petrol dumps at the Hartenstein were hit. Fires were started and Lieutenant Storrs organized a party to put them out between bursts of fixed trajectory mortaring. A jeep carrying small arms and some six-pounder ammunition were the next casualties, causing bullets to shoot in all directions. Sapper Brimble, Sgt Cooper and Staff Sgt Brown all had a lucky escape when trying to get this under control by shoveling earth onto it. Incoming mortars were heard and the three jumped into the same trench, when the six-pounder ammunition blew up, completely destroying the jeep.[41]

Captain Green was woken at 1200 hours by Henniker's batman, Sapper Meck, and given something to eat. Next he was driven to the General's HQ for a 13:30 meeting. Captain Green: *"I explained to the General the desperate situation at Arnhem and that they could not hold out much longer. He agreed that they would push ahead immediately with the Canadian Engineers and their boats to try and evacuate our troops across the river. I spent the rest of the afternoon briefing the Engineers about the river and the river banks."* [42]

At 1430 hours, Captain Green crossed the Nijmegen bridge to join the column that was trying to break through. Previously at 1300 hours, the Irish Guards of the Guards Armoured Division begun to advance from the bridgehead north of the Waal River. Ten minutes after they had started, three of the leading Sherman tanks were hit by German guns and set on fire. With the attack halted, Captain Green returned to Corps HQ to contact the Chief Engineer.[43]

By now General Urquhart got definite information that XXX Corps was held up north of Nijmegen, but that they were attempting to push through to Driel where the 1st Independent Polish Parachute Brigade had just landed, with an armoured column with supplies for the 1st Airborne Division. Unfortunately, all contact with the troops on the Arnhem bridge had ceased. There was also no news that Captains Green or Malden had made contact. It was assumed that they had been captured. The General didn't know that Green was actually part of the column trying to advance from the Nijmegen bridgehead. Nor did her knew that, unfortunately, the Guards Armoured Brigade were held up by enemy 88mm guns so they couldn't advance.

Lieutenant Sankey asked Myers for more of an active role and at 1840 hours he was sent to take command of a party from the 10th Battalion, The Parachute Regiment covering a road block from the direction of Arnhem. At 2130 hours Lieutenant Storrs and a battle-weary party of 9 Field Company went down to the river with all the jeep trailers that they could muster, in an attempt to ferry some of the Polish Parachute Brigade from the South bank of the Neder Rijn into our own perimeter. Lieutenant-Colonel Myers: *"During the night, I went down to the river myself. The current was too strong for operating these rafts made of jeep trailers lashed together, and just before dawn we had to give up."* [44]

At 2300 hours Green attended a conference held by Lieutenant-Colonel Henniker to give information on river banks for a proposed assault crossing.

Not much good news came with daylight on the 22nd. Sapper Brimble, *"German mortar fire and bullets from fixed-point machine gun fire bombarded the area frequently. The ground was very sandy which caused the magazines of the airborne troops' Sten Guns to become blocked and need constant cleaning. During the morning of the 22nd, mortar fire destroyed one of the HQRE jeeps, a motorcycle and much of the units equipment and stores. It also set fire to the fuel dump for a second time."* [45]

Lieutenant Storrs again led the party to put out the fire. [46]

With no news from Captains Green or Malden, General Urquhart told Mackenzie that he wanted him to go over to Browning and Horrocks to make their situation unmistakably known and also to find out all he could about the efforts and whereabouts of the relief force. General Urquhart: *"It's necessary that they should know that the division no longer exists as such and that we are now merely a collection of individuals holding on'. Mackenzie, a slightly built Scot with an air about him of immense responsibility, covered up whatever misgivings he may have harboured about such a hair-raising mission. `Make clear to them,*

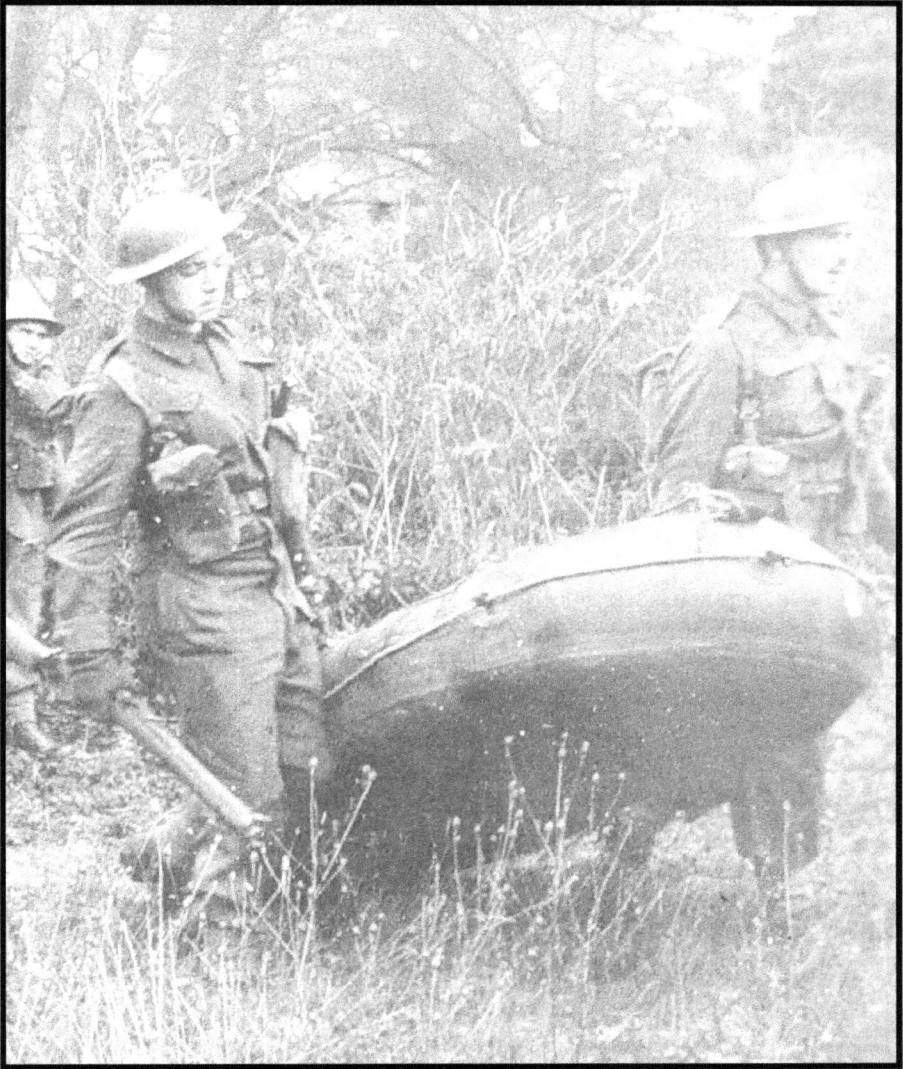

Above: during a training mission two men easily carry a reconnaissance boat. This is the type of boat that Lieutenant Storrs rowed across the fast moving Lower Rhine River.

(Author's collection)

Charles,' I added, `that we're terribly short of men, ammunition, food and medical supplies, and that we need some DUKWs to ferry the Poles across. If supplies don't arrive tonight it may be too late.' The ferrying arrangements would soon need priority, and their specialist nature suggested that it would be useful also to send Eddie Myers, a most able engineer, with Machenzie." [47]

Lieutenant-Colonel Myers handed over command to Major Jack Winchester. *"There was little to hand over. All the sappers except three men of HQRE were in different sectors of the firing line."* [48]

At 1210 hours, Myers and Mackenzie left to make contact with the Poles and 43rd Division and crossed the river under cover of a certain amount of fog via a raft rowed by Lieutenant Storrs. They crossed the Neder Rijn about 150 yards to the west of the railway bridge on which the enemy were sitting.

The crossing was surprisingly uneventful. *"Only a few shots were fired at us,"* Mackenzie said, *"And they went over our heads."* [49]

Urquhart received word of their safe crossing at 1350 hours. Meckenzie and Myers made contact with the British Liaison Officer to the Polish Brigade at a pre-arranged rendezvous in an orchard on the South bank of the river and eventually, having by-passed the enemy, they safely reached Polish Brigade Headquarters in the village of Driel. They told Sosabowski that some small rubber boats were being prepared on the north bank to get as many Poles across. It was the CRE idea to use the two-man rubber dinghies and link them by hawser so they could be pulled back and forth across the river. This is based on the principal that the British Assault boat Mark III could be operated by, but unfortunately they didn't have proper roping or the Assault boats to make it work.[50]

At 1440 hours Major Winchester arrived to take command of the HQRE amongst the mortaring and shelling. Shortly after his arrival, the War Diary reported that what was left of the rations was now finished. I am sure that there is no connection between the arrival of Major Winchester and the end of the rations.

The new plan for the 30 Corps' advance was for the 43rd Wessex Division to by-pass the heavy resistance at Elst by hooking around to the west and the north to Driel. It took all day for the

Above: two DUKWs come ashore. Even though they didn't require any docking facilities, they still required a relatively flat area to come ashore. Even thought it could climb a 60% grade and broach a 18" high obstacle, the high river beds and mud of the Lower Rhine River were to prove to be a problem for the few DUKWs that were launched.

DUKW Specifications:
Length: 31 feet
Width: 8'-2.9"
Height: 8'-9.5"
Weight: 19,570 pounds
Maximum Land Speed: 45 mph
Maximum Water Speed: 6.3 mph

The DUKW 353 series was the U.S. Army's amphibious version of their 2 1/2 ton truck. D stood for built in 1942, U for amphibious 2 1/2 ton truck, K was for front wheel drive and W was for real wheel drive.

infantry of 43rd Wessex Division to take Oosterhout. This delayed a mixed column of a squadron of tanks and a mobile detachment of a battalion of 43 Division, together with two DUKWs loaded with urgently needed ammunition and supplies, setting out for Driel. The column was divided into two columns. The first consisted of `A' Squadron of the 4/7 Dragoon Guards and the armoured vehicles of the 5th Duke of Cornwall's Light Infantry. The second column consisted of all the soft skin vehicles and the rest of the infantry battalion. The two DUKWs were with the second column.[51]

By 22:00 hours Oosterhout was clear and the way was open for these columns to move forward. Captain Green travelled with their leading tanks, which were to force a passage for the amphibious vehicles. The column was held up two miles west of Elst by 88mm guns, Captain Green and the Sergeant went through enemy lines on foot to get back to Driel.

Captain Green: *"By midnight the leading troops had been stopped by a German patrol and the leading tank destroyed, as the roads were bordered by deep dikes the vehicles could not get off the road. It was clear that further advance was going to take time, so I decided it would be best to leave the convoy and make my way on foot, so I went back into the fields and dikes and trekked through the night arriving back at Driel at dawn. It was too dangerous to cross back over the river during the day so I hid up until dark."* [52]

As this was happening, at 2300 hours the crossing began and Major Winchester thought that the Poles were being ferried over on six two-man reconnaissance boats and one unwieldy RAF dinghy at a rate of sixteen per hour.

Lieutenant-Colonel Myers: *"That night, the 22nd September, with all the recce boats that could be mustered from the North bank and rafts made by the Polish Engineers, under pretty unpleasant and continuous fire, we attempted again to get elements of the Polish Brigade across into our own perimeter on the North bank of the Neder Rijn. We failed to get a line across the river. A good many Poles floated down into the enemy lines. But, largely as a result of the magnificent personal efforts of David Storrs, who, with his own hands, rowed twenty-three trips across the river that night, we succeeded in getting a total of about sixty Poles across."*
[53]

Above: a typical loading diagram of the Assault Boat Mark III, showing the positioning of the crew and passengers. (from: Field Engineering and Mine Warfare Pamphlet No. 8 Part I (All arms) Assault River Crossing)

Below: Canadian Scottish training in a Mark III Assault Boat during a training exercise in the U.K.. (National Archives and Library of Canada)

The war diary reports that he made twenty-six trips and others say a different number. I am sure that even Lieutenant Storrs was unaware of how many trips he made. Whatever the number of trips, he went beyond the call of duty.[54]

Unfortunately the two DUKWs loaded with supplies never reached the river. While en route to the river they both slid on the wet cobbled road and became stuck. Neither one was able to cross the river.

Early the next morning, the 23rd September, Charles Mackenzie and Myers left, each in an armoured car, to try to get through to 30 Corps Headquarters at Nijmegen. They had not been going more than a mile when Mackenzie's armoured car, which was in the lead, got a direct hit from a German half-track which was lying in wait, watching the road. The occupants of the armoured car safely bailed out. But before they did so, they sent a hurried message, over the radio to go back for reinforcements. They returned to Driel and, thirty minutes later with a troop of tanks, set out again for the South. There was no sign by then of Mackenzie or of the rest of the armoured car crew. He eventually got through to Nijmegen to XXX Corps Headquarters, where he explained the situation.

In the afternoon, when Mackenzie eventually caught up with Myers at Browning's HQ, he was so weary, wet and shivering that a hot bath was produced to thaw him out before business could be discussed. Unfortunately, he doubted whether he conveyed the seriousness of the situation at Arnhem. He saw no urgency in either XXX Corps or 43rd Division HQ.[55]

Interesting, there is no mention of Captain Green by either Horrocks or Henniker in their memoirs. I guess that the Captain was too junior for them to write about.

At 0830 hours, Captain Green got to Driel and contacted Lieutenant-Colonel Myers. Having briefed everybody as to the situation and given all the information they could, and after having warmed themselves with food and whisky generously supplied both by XXX Corps and Airborne Corps Headquarters and with some dry clothes on, they set off later in the afternoon. Lieutenant-Colonel Myers slept most of the way. Under the arrangement of Major Winchester, Mackenzie crossed back into the Oosterbeek Perimeter in the night. Lieutenant Storrs took him across by dinghy at 2300 hours. The Lieutenant seemed to have become the division's ferryman. The CRE waited in order to brief the engineers of 43rd Division of their plan to ferry the 130 Infantry Brigade which was then moving up towards Driel, as they spoke over the river. As he waited, there was another attempt to transport the Poles across the River. This time it was with assault boats which had been lent by 130 Infantry Brigade and which were manned by Polish Airborne Engineers. Approximately two hundred more Poles were taken across the river.[56]

Lieutenant-Colonel Myers on the Polish crossing, *"I can find no fault with their attempts; they did as much as they could. They had not been trained in river crossings, and the Arnhem plan had not envisaged one, and no one had any proper boats. But the less said about their watermanship the better".* [57]

The CRE had to endure another sleepless night under continuous fire of the enemy eighty-one millimeter mortars. Meanwhile north of the Neder Rijn, German 88mm shelling started at 0400 hours, two hours earlier than normal. At 07:30 German mortars joined in. The second HQRE jeep was blown up along with the remainder of the stores and the radio set. The War Diary reported that all contact with the units was lost.[58]

Sadly, Lieutenant Crofton E. Peter Sankey was shot in the chest by a sniper while defending the roadblock and died instantly. His field grave was close to where he was shot. It was in the garden of the Berghege family which was on the Utrechtsweg opposite of Annastraat.[59]

On the 24th the HQRE position was mortared continually during the night to about 03:00 and then Spandau MG fire was trained on the hotel grounds. At 0729 hours very heavy mortaring and shelling commenced and another HQRE motorcycle was destroyed. The Hotel grounds were now completely in shambles and at 1427 hours, the HQ area came under fire from a German machine gun on the hospital and from snipers.[60]

South of the river, the CRE attended another conference at 130 Brigade Headquarters. They were planning a brigade attack into the Western area of the perimeter, which eventually evolved into a plan for only one battalion to perform an assault crossing because there were not sufficient assault boats for more than that.[61]

At 2330 hours, after waiting all day for it to get dark, Captain

Green made an unsuccessful attempt to cross the river.

About twenty DUKWs loaded with food, medical supplies and ammunition had reached Driel, and Lieutenant-Colonel Myers decided to get across the Rijn that night behind the battalion of 130 Brigade, to get these supplies, so sorely needed, to 1 Airborne Division. Myers: *"I had planned to cross at the ferry site at Heaveadorp – the only place where was a ramp both sides of the river – as soon as it was recaptured by the assaulting battalion of 130 Brigade. But the attack went all wrong, and at 1 o'clock in the morning, having discovered that there was, anyhow, a more or less safe approach to the South side of the ferry, although the far side was still in enemy hands and there was a certain amount of fire coming straight across the river, I decided to move up these unwieldy DUKWs from Driel. I was carrying a letter which had just arrived from General Browning, Commander 1 Airborne Corps. It was for General Urquhart, the GOC 1 Airborne Division. Its contents, which I had memorized, gave instructions to General Urquhart to withdraw the survivors of 1 Airborne Division the following night if this night's attack did not succeed in relieving the situation. I ordered the DUKWs forward. As the first one, loaded with ammunition, slithered into the water, a stream of light automatic fire swept under its belly. We got two safely into the river. I jumped on the third; it was the last to get across. We reached the North bank about a hundred yards below the site, only to discover that the infantry of the battalion of 130 Brigade, who had all crossed by then, were held up by strong enemy fire right on the banks of the river. I told the RASC NCO in charge of the DUKWs which had already crossed, to wait where he was until daylight, and to bring the DUKWs with the Divisional perimeter as soon as the enlargement of the battalion bridgehead allowed him safe movement. I decided that I must get on to my own Divisional Headquarters in view of the importance of the message which I carried; for I knew, from what I had seen already, that the attack would not relieve the situation in the perimeter."* [62]

The CRE was bent over so as to avoid the pot shots of the enemy because of his noisy (his words not mine) movements. He clambered along in the water under the north bank of the river until he knew he was within the perimeter. He eventually got back to British 1st Airborne Divisional Headquarters about 0600 hours in the morning and, having delivered the message to General Urquhart, he resumed command from Jack Winchester. 'Resumed' was hardly the word, which was merciful because the CRE was exhausted.[63]

The message that the CRE brought back for the General was:

> *Dear Roy:*
>
>> *Sosabowski will be bringing you this, I hope to-night.*
>
>> *I will not labour your present position, and it may be little consolation to you and the 1st Division when I tell you that the opinion held this side of the river is that the action of the 1st Division has, apart from the killing of the many Boche it has undoubtedly achieved, enabled XXX*

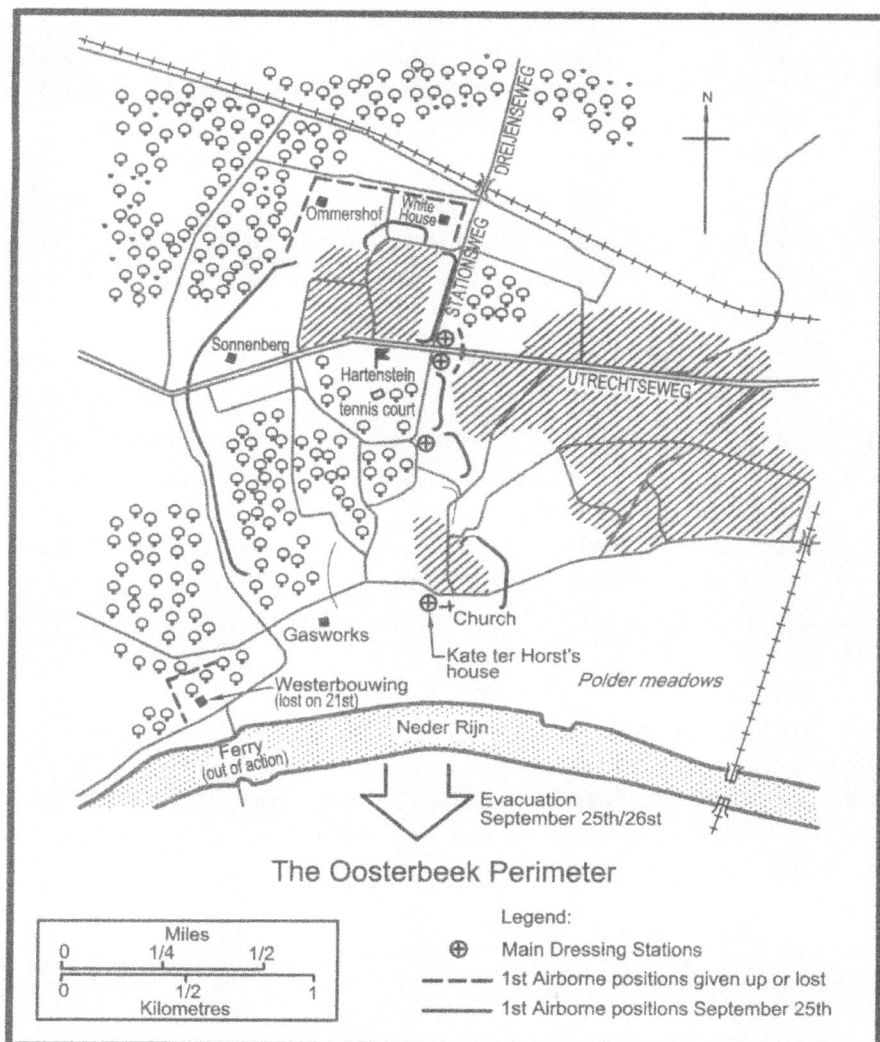

The Oosterbeek Perimeter

Legend:
⊕   Main Dressing Stations
– – – –   1st Airborne positions given up or lost
————   1st Airborne positions September 25th

Corps and the Airborne Corps between them to capture the Nijmegen bridges and to break clean through the main German defense line on the Waal.

From the information at our disposal, the Germans undoubtedly moved back the bulk of his forces from Nijmegen to Arnhem just before our airborne attack took place, and instead of the Nijmegen crossings being an acutely difficult problem, the Arnhem crossings have become most acute in consequence.

You can rest assured that XXX Corps are doing their maximum under the most appalling difficulties to relieve you. As you know, I am responsible for from inclusive Nijmegen down the narrow corridor back for approximately 40 miles, and the road has been cut between us and the main body for 24 hours, which does not help matters much. It is now through again, and the Army is pouring to your assistance but, as you will appreciate better than I do, very late in the day.

I naturally feel, not so tired and frustrated as you do, but probably almost worse about the whole thing than you do.

I enclose a copy of a letter from Field Marshal Monty, [no letter was enclosed] and I hope to see you in a day or two.

It may amuse you to know that my front faces in all directions, but I am only in close contact with the enemy for about 8000 yards to the south-east, which is quite enough in present circumstances.

Yours ever,

F.A.M. Browning.[64]

The mortar fire had been heavy since 0600 hours and it destroyed the remaining motorcycles, meaning that the HQRE was now completely without transport. At 0830 hours Captain Green contacted Myers by wireless and received orders to remain in his present location in Driel.[65]

The Last River Crossing

General Urquhart held a conference in the cellar of the Harten-stein. Lieutenant-Colonel Myers was one of those present and he looked just as exhausted as the other senior officers there. The General said, *"We are to clear out tonight."* Then he explained that units would withdraw on a timed program by two routes. *"In general those farthest from the river will start first. I don't expect that either of the routes will be free from enemy interference, but they are the best available to us."* [66]

The plan included the posting of glider pilots acting as guides on both the east and west routes as far as the open marshy land alongside the river. In difficult places the routes were marked with parachute tape. Guides from each unit made themselves familiar with the routes during the day. It was left to Lieutenant-Colonel Myers and his sappers to look after the last sketches to the embarkation points. Men were to move in boatload parties of fourteen with their boots muffled and would take evasive action if engaged, and only retaliate if it was vital.

General Urquhart: *"On Myers fell the dual responsibility of selecting the routes and fixing the ferry service. He had hardly recovered from his ordeal of crossing the river in both directions only a little time before. Yet he managed to look extremely alert and he was, as usual, full of ideas. There was no need to underline just how vital were his technical experience and his qualities of character to the division's survival."* [67]

On the north shore, Lieutenant-Colonel Henniker oversaw the launching of Operation Berlin, the evacuation of the British 1st Airborne Division. Mark Henniker on his reaction seeing the first boats go: *"They vanished into the inky darkness. There was nothing to be seen and nothing seemed to be happening. I paced the shore concealing, I hope, the inevitable doubts that assailed me. Had the Sappers upset the boats and all gone silently to the bottom? Had they paddled their boats into waiting Germans, concealed on the far bank? Had the boats been washed downstream to God knows where? It was a tense interval and no man could have importuned his Maker more fervently than I did that night."* He didn't know how long it was, but then he heard the sound of dipping paddles. *"Then I saw a boat. It held a dozen men. I could recognize their airborne-pattern helmets. What a welcome sight it was!"* [68]

Captain Green, *"By night fall, some boats had arrived with the Canadian Engineers, I crossed the river by the first boat available and met Lt Col Myers on the other bank. The troops were filtering down to the river from Oosterbeek as our perimeter defenses were holding the Germans back. 30 Corps artillery put down a creeping barrage over the heads of the retreating troops keeping the Germans back."* [69]

At 2030 hours the HQRE moved down to the river bank. During the journey, the CRE and one sapper were slightly wounded by shrapnel. The river was reached safely, helped by heavy rainfall. Sapper Brimble managed to get in a boat and crossed to the south bank of the river, still with full kit, including his Sten gun. By 2115 all of the HQRE were completely across the river.[70]

Waiting for them was Lieutenant-Colonel Henniker: *"I met many old friends: General Urquhart, Eddie Myers and many sappers tramped past in the dark. The plan was working."* [71]

Lieutenant-Colonel Myers on Mark Henniker: *"He and his men did a grand job for us that night."* [72]

General Urquhart: *"As we strode out along the road beyond the dyke, Roberts and I were challenged in the dark by a familiar voice. It was that of Colonel Henniker, the 43rd Division's chief engineer who had previously been with the 1st Airborne Division. He was wearing a ground sheet, and a tin hat to keep off the rain. He appeared to be optimistic about the progress of the evacuation."* [73]

And indeed he should have been. His plan worked.

Headquarters, Airborne Divisional Engineers War Establishment

(i) Personnel   (as of March 1945)

Commander, R.E. (lieutenant-colonel)	1
Adjutant (captain)	1
Field (subaltern)	1
Intelligence officer (subaltern)	1
Total officers	4
Regimental serjeant-major	1
Clerk	1
Total, warrant officers and serjeants	2
Tradesman (includes 1 corporal + 1 lance-corporal)	
Clerks	2
Draughtsman (topographical)	1
Pioneers for duty as -	
General dutymen (trained as drivers, IC)	2
Medical officer's orderly (lance-corporal)	1
Motorcyclists	2
Total, tradesmen	8
Non-tradesman (includes 1 lance-corporal)	
Drivers, I.C. for duty as -	
Drivers of vehicles	1
Batmen	1
Batman-driver	2
Total, non-tradesmen (includes 1 lance-corporal)	4
Total, other rank and file	12
Total, other ranks	14
Total, headquarters airborne divisional engineers	18
Attached -	
RAMC - Medical officer	1
REME - Captain	1
APTC - Instructor	1
Total, attached	3
Total, headquarters airborne divisional engineers	21

Above and over: because of the lessons learned at Arnhem, War Establishments were revamped. This was put into effect as the division regrouped.

After Arnhem

The following morning Sapper Brimble met his former CRE Col. Henniker who recognized Sapper Brimble's voice and came over to speak to him. The evacuees were temporarily accommodated in a church hall at Driel. They were then taken to Nijmegen by truck, and then onto Louvain in Belguim from where they were flown on the 29th home to England. They arrived at 1930 hours at Barksten Heath and the HQRE was re-established in Fulbeck Manor near Granthan, Lincs.[74]

Eddie Myers wrote an article that stated numerous reasons why the operation failed and most of these have been covered before in other books and are now considered fact. I will only include only the reasons that pertain to the R.E. or problems he saw first hand. He wrote: *"The only river crossing equipment we had brought in by air was some half a dozen two-men inflatable reconnaissance boats. The current proved too strong for rafts made up out of jeep trailers. To transfer more than a few Poles across the Rhine, by then only possible by night, we were therefore entirely dependent on XXX Corps for additional ferrying equipment. The three-fold effect of arriving piecemeal, so far from the main-road bridge, and over a period of five days, resulted in our never*

	Airborne	Base
(ii) Transport		
Bicycle	0	1
Bicycle, folding	2	0
Motor-cycles, folding	2	0
Motor-cycles, heavy	0	4
Car, 4-seater, 4x2	0	1
Cars, 5-cwt, 4x4	2	0
Truck, 15-cwt, 4x2, G.S.	0	1
Trailers, 10-cwt	2	0
Lorry, 3-ton, 4x4, office	0	1
Trailers, 1-ton, 2-wheeled, GS	0	1
(iii) Weapons		
Light machine gun, .303-inch		1
Projector, infantry, anti-tank		1
Pistol, signal		1

being in a position effectively to reinforce the one Brigade allocated to our primary task on D-day until too late. By then the enemy had surrounded the rest of the Division. This underwrote our disaster.

"Lastly, it is regrettably necessary to elaborate on the lack of any apparent urgency by XXX Corps. As a result of a most gallant assault crossing of the river Waal at Nijmegen by a Combat Regiment of 82 Airborne Division, the road and railway bridges there were captured intact on the afternoon of 20 September. The forward elements of XXX Corps were then only eleven miles and one major river obstacle away from 1st Airborne Division. And yet, four clear days later, XXX Corps was still unable to launch 43rd Division across the Rhine in sufficient strength to relieve us. This has always seemed to me to have been inexcusable. When I left XXX Corps HQ with Charles Mackenzie on the afternoon of 24 September on our way back to our Division HQ, I was given to understand that, if we did not succeed in getting a sufficiently large part of the Polish Para Brigade across the Rhine that night in about a dozen assault boats which XXX Corps were managing to send up to Driel that day, the whole 43rd Division, the then leading Division of XXX Corps, was to come to our help across the Rhine the following night."[75]

Since the Poles weren't ferried over in sufficient number, he expected there to be a major assault by the 43rd Division. There wasn't: *"...when I attended the Orders Group for the attack, I discovered that the force had been whittled down to one Battalion, 4 Dorsets...But even if there were only enough Assault Boats for an initial attack by one Battalion, there should have been enough still afloat after the assault for a further Battalion to follow them."*[76]

He ended on a personal note: *"The nine-day Battle of Arnhem certainly enabled me to learn a bit more about myself, in that it tested my powers of endurance to their limit. Almost constant shelling and mortaring, added to rifle and especially enemy sniper fire – at which they were adept – is horrible at any time, especially so day after day and much of the nights. But when, in addition, one has been desperately short of sleep and short of food for several days on end, the effort to remain alert and to be able to think and lead is tremendous."*[77]

Eddie Myers was awarded the Dutch Bronze Lion and served in the Far East soon after Arnhem. He was promoted to Colonel when he served in Korea. Leter, promoted to Brigadier, he was the Chief Engineer, British Troops in Egypt 1955-56. Next he was the Deputy Director Personnel Administration, War Office from 1956 to 1959. He retired from the army and worked for various private companies until he retired in 1971. He passed away in 1997.

In 1947 Mark Henniker went to India to command a mixed Anglo-Indian Engineer regiment in the Punjab during the tempestuous upheavals in the Partition of India. After, he was an instructor at the School of Military Engineering at Chatham until he was promoted to Brigadier and given the 63 Gurkha Infantry Brigade to command. They fought in the Malayan Jungles from 1952 to 1954. His last military appointment was as Commander Corps Royal Engineer of the 1st British Corps in Germany 1955-58. During his service he was awarded the CBE, OBE, DSO and MC. He died in 1991.

Roll of Honour

Lieutenant Crofton E. Peter Sankey

251037; age 21. Killed on September 23rd and is buried in Oosterbeek.

After Word

Ironically, the group of engineers that was raised and trained by Mark Henniker and then turned over to Eddie Myers was evacuated by four RE and RCE companies under Mark Henniker's command. It was a strange twist of fate and the evacuation was one of the few things that went right during Operation Market Garden.

Because of the speed that Operation Market Garden was planned by the division certain details were missed, and probably the most glaring oversight was the Heavendorp Ferry. If everything had gone according to plan then the ferry would not have been a factor, but since the operation went wrong the ferry was to prove to be a gross oversight. Lt-Col. Myers: *"The divisional staff, including myself I freely admit, did not realize how important the ferry would become."* [78]

This led to the biggest problem facing the HQRE; how to get men and equipment across a fast moving river. The extraordinary efforts by Lieutenant Storrs to paddle men across the river wasn't enough. The failure was a case of simple logic missed by Eddie Myers and his staff. Would Mark Henniker have realized if you land by a river then boats of some kind were needed? I think so because the thing about his personality that got him kicked out of the Airborne was exactly the critical eye that was needed. I am pretty sure that he would have looked at the Operation Market Garden plan and like Brigadier Hackett, could see the flaws in it and prepare for the worse. His pessimism would have made sure that they had brought boats.

In their defense, Eddie Myers and his staff had the distraction of still trying to get to know each other during the planning of the operation. A good working relationship takes time. As decorated and competent as he was, Eddie Myers had never planned an operation on this scale. Granted during the first few days most of his sappers were "borrowed" by the brigades, so he never had to plan their part in any detail. It was later that his main job would have kicked in. Unfortunately, things never went according to plan and Myers was forced into roles that he didn't think that he would find himself in. In these, he excelled wonderfully! His experience in Yugoslavia paid off.

The flaw of the RE plan is what wasn't in it. Only once did it mention boats and that was if all of the bridging were destroyed. Also, it had the Field Park Company acting only as the RE stores dump. Yes, this task was a big part of their usual job, but so was supplying stores like bridging and supplying technical support for heavy machinery like barges. Unfortunately, because of the shortage of gliders, these parts of the field park company were left back in England.

The plan was based on capturing at least one bridge and because of this the RE plan was as flawed as the overall plan and hence, both were victims of the over-optimistic spirit that plagued the division at the time. No contingency plan was properly developed in case no bridges were captured.

No wonder the river became a major problem. In Lessons from Arnhem, Myers seemed to have learned this lesson. He wrote: *"Had the Airborne Div had 30 assault boats available two nights earlier, sufficient sappers could have been mustered to get the whole of the Polish Brigade across in one night. Had the sappers been equipped with a line rocket firing apparatus, (necessary for impoverished ferrying across the broad rivers of Europe and for effectively making serial ropeways across the gorges of Burma and the Far East), many more Poles could have been got across. But in the planning of the operation it was envisaged that when the Poles would be dropped South of the river, we would have been in possession of the Arnhem main bridge. Bad WT communication prevented any last minute alteration of their dropping area, and were then in possession of no area suitable for bringing in assault boats by glider."*[79]

What Myers and his staff lost in planning, they made up in the field. Here, Eddie Myers gets full marks. He crossed the river to tell the generals of how badly things were going, was part of the relief column and in the end was in charge of the north bank of the evacuation. The failures from this point had nothing to do with him.

Correspondingly, Mark Henniker had even less time to get to know his sappers and was also given a responsibility that wasn't in the original plan. His planning and execution of Operation Berlin was sound, especially under the circumstances.

Both CRE of the British 1st Airborne Division were outstanding officers who in the end worked well with each other to save what was left of the battered division. Each had their strengths and weaknesses and it was no coincidence that both of their careers advanced after Arnhem.

End Notes

1 - An Image of War
2 - p71 An Image of War
3 – An Image of War
4 – Green's Account
5 - p165 An Image of War
6 - pp165-166 An Image of War
7- Middlebrook
8 - p127 Royal Engineers Battlefield Tour
9 – CRE orders
10 – Sankey's orders
11 – Green's Account
12 - Green's Account
13 – Green's Account
14 - Brimble's Account / Lessons From Arnhem / War Diary / A Bridge Too Far
15 - p127 Royal Engineers Battlefield Tour
16 - p127 Royal Engineers Battlefield Tour
17 - p127 Royal Engineers Battlefield Tour
18 - Brimble's Account
19 - War Diary / Middlebrook / p189 Then and Now
20 - p127 Royal Engineers Battlefield Tour
21 - War Diary / Brimble's Account
22 - p128 Royal Engineers Battlefield Tour
23 - p128 Royal Engineers Battlefield Tour / War Diary
24 – Then and now / Green's Account
25 – Green's Account
26 – Green's Account
27 – Brimble's Account / War Diary
28 – p128 Royal Engineers Battlefield Tour / War Diary
29 – p128 Royal Engineers Battlefield Tour
30 – Green's Account
31 – Brimble's Account
32 – Lessons From Arnhem
33 – p128 Royal Engineers Battlefield Tour
34 – p128 Royal Engineers Battlefield Tour / Urquhart / 1st ABN HQ War Diary
35 – War Diary
36 – Green's Account
37 – Green's Account
38 – Green's Account
39 – p166 An Image of War
40 – p166 An Image of War
41 – War Diary /Brimble' s Account / Citation Green
42 - Green's Account
43 - Then and Now
44 - p128 Royal Engineers Battlefield Tour
45 - Brimble's Account
46 - Citation Green
47 - p143 Urquhart
48 - p128 Royal Engineers Battlefield Tour
49 - A Bridge Too Far
50 - A Bridge Too Far / Engineers at the Bridge / pp128/9 Royal Engineers Battlefield Tour / Middlebrook
51 - pp128-129 Royal Engineers Battlefield Tour
52 - Green's Account
53 - p129 Royal Engineers Battlefield Tour
54 - War Diary
55 - p129 Royal Engineers Battlefield Tour / War Diary
56 - Green's Account / War Diary
57 - Middlebrook
58 - p129 Royal Engineers Battlefield Tour / Brimble's Account / War Diary
59 - Brimble's Account / Roll of Honour / War Diary
60 - War Diary
61 - p129 Royal Engineers Battlefield Tour
62 - p129 Royal Engineers Battlefield Tour
63 - pp129-130 Royal Engineers Battlefield Tour
64 - Urquhart
65 - War Diary
66 - Urquhart p130 Royal Engineers Battlefield Tour
67 - pp175-176 Urquhart
68 - p192 An Image of War
69 - Green's Account
70 - War Diary / Brimble's Account
71 - p192 An Image of War
72 - p130 Royal Engineers Battlefield Tour
73 - p184 Urquhart
74 - Middlebrooke / Brimble's Account
75 - Lessons from Arnhem
76 - Lessons from Arnhem
77 - Lessons from Arnhem
78 - Middlebrook
79 - Lessons from Arnhem

Sources

`At Arnhem September 1944' Brigadier E.C. Myers CBE, DSO, BA, C Eng. MICE

Royal Engineers Battlefield Tour: The Seine to the Rhine Volume 1

`The Battle Of Arnhem Personal Recollections After 30 Years' by Major Michael D. Green, R.E., T.D.

CRE 1 Airborne Div Op Instruction No. 1

Account: Sapper V.H. Brimble

`Lessons From Arnhem' by Myers

`An Image Of War' by Mark Henniker

`Arnhem' by Major-General Urquhart CB, DSO

`Arnhem' by Martin Middlebrook

`DUKW in Action' Squadron/Signal Publications

`The Island' by Tim Saunders

`Who Was Who During the Battle of Arnhem' C. van Roekel

`Urquhart of Arnhem' by John Baynes

`Arnhem' by Major-General Urquhart CB, DSO

War Diary Headquarter Royal Engineers

1st Abn HQ War Diary

`A Bridge Too Far' by C. Ryan

`Then and Now' by After the Battle

Index

Lowe, L/Cpl; 5,29

Mackenzie, Lt-Col; 6,32,34,38,47
Malden, Capt. C.P.; 26,31
Meek, Sap; 5,29,31
Murray, Maj; 23
Myers, Lt-Col. Eddie; 1,8,9,12,14,17,19,20,22-24,26,28,31,34,36,
          38-40,42-44,48-50

O'Callaghan; 24

Sankey, Lt. C.E.P.; 5-7,9,14,16,17,19,24,32,39,48
Storrs, Lt. David; 5-7,9,17,20,24,31,34,38

Tickell, General; 30
Thomas, Major General G.I.; 30

Urquhart, Major General Roy; 6-8,29,31,34,40,41,43,44

Winchester, Major; 1,24,34,36,40

Young, Major General B.K.; 2

About The Author

John Sliz became fascinated with Operation Market Garden after he read, `A Bridge Too Far' at the age of nine. Many years later, a visit to Arnhem in the summer of 2001 only added fuel to the fire, eventually resulting in the publication of his first book, `The Storm Boat Kings'. While researching this book and waiting for its publication, he wrote a small booklet on the engineer equipment that was used during the operation. `Engineer Assault Boats In Canadian Service' was published in December 2006.

Since then he has written the first seven books of the Market Garden Engineer Series. He currently lives in Toronto, Ontario and is busy researching engineers in World War II. For more information or to contact him please visit: www.stormboatkings.ca

Other Military Books By The Same Author

By Vanwell Publishing: (www.vanwell.com)
The Storm Boat Kings: The 23rd Royal Canadian Engineers At Arnhem 1944

By Service Publications: (www.servicepub.com)
Non-Bailey Bridging In Canadian Service
Engineer Assault Boats In Canadian Service
The Bailey Bridge In Canadian Service

Market Garden Engineer Series: (www.stormboatkings.ca)

#1) The Wrong Side Of The River: The Polish Engineer Company At Arnhem

#2) Basic Function: The 4th Parachute Squadron, Royal Engineers At Arnhem

#3) Engineers At The Bridge: The 1st Parachute Squadron Royal Engineers At Arnhem

#4) Assault Boats On The Waal: The 307th Engineer Battalion During Operation Market Garden

#5) Bridging Hell's Highway: The 326th Engineer Battalion During Operation Market Garden

#6) A Long Tradition: The 9th (Airborne) Field Company Royal Engineers At Arnhem

#7) A Token Force: The 261st Field Park Company Royal Engineers (Airborne) At Arnhem

#8) Commander Royal Engineers: The Headquarters of the Royal Engineers at Arnhem

Allied Assault Boats: A Study of the Assault and Storm Boats Used in River Crossings in Europe During World War II

Encyclopedia of the R.C.E. In WWII: Part One: The Field Units

www.ingramcontent.com/pod-product-compliance
Lightning Source LLC
Chambersburg PA
CBHW071641040426
42452CB00009B/1718